Native American Tribes: The History and Culture of the Mound Builders

By Charles River Editors

The Grave Creek Mound in present-day Moundsville, West Virginia is believed to have been built by the Adena

About Charles River Editors

Charles River Editors was founded by Harvard and MIT alumni to provide superior editing and original writing services, with the expertise to create digital content for publishers across a vast range of subject matter. In addition to providing original digital content for third party publishers, Charles River Editors republishes civilization's greatest literary works, bringing them to a new generation via ebooks.

Introduction

Monks Mound, built circa 950-1100 A.D. in present-day Collinsville, Illinois.

The Mound Builders

"There being one of these [mounds] in my neighborhood, I wished to satisfy myself whether any, and which of these opinions [regarding the identity of the Mound Builders] were just. For this purpose I determined to open and examine it thoroughly." – Thomas Jefferson

From the "Trail of Tears" to Wounded Knee and Little Bighorn, the narrative of American history is incomplete without the inclusion of the Native Americans that lived on the continent before European settlers arrived in the 16th and 17th centuries. Since the first contact between natives and settlers, tribes like the Sioux, Cherokee, and Navajo have both fascinated and perplexed outsiders with their history, language, and culture. In Charles River Editors' Native American Tribes series, readers can get caught up to speed on the history and culture of North America's most famous native tribes in the time it takes to finish a commute, while learning interesting facts long forgotten or never known.

When Europeans first came upon the giant mounds and earthworks dotting the North American landscape in the 18th century, they couldn't imagine that American "Indians" were capable of such advanced technology and masterful engineering. In fact, when President George Washington sent adventurer and military strategist Rufus Putnam to survey the land at the convergence of the Ohio and Muskingum Rivers in southeastern Ohio for settlement, Putnam reported that he'd discovered an impressive walled earthwork complex near present-day Marietta that was obviously the breastwork of an ancient fortress built by some long-forgotten ancient civilization. Like others of his time, Putnam couldn't conceive that indigenous Americans had at one time reached such an advanced level of cultural and technical sophistication.

As detailed by Thomas Jefferson in his 1783 book, Notes on the State of Virginia, about 1780 the future American President began to excavate a mound near Monticello, his Virginia estate. He noted, "I determined to open and examine it thoroughly. It was situated on the low grounds of the Rivanna [River], about two miles above its principal fork, and opposite to some hills, on which had been an Indian town. It was of a spheroidical form, of about 40 feet diameter at the base." Jefferson discovered stratified human remains and ultimately concluded that this particular mound was an ancient Indian burial place. Credited with what was perhaps the first systematic archaeological excavation in North America, Jefferson came to the realization that different mounds might serve different uses, which has since been proven correct.

However, even as these elaborate earthen complexes have ultimately yielded tens of thousands of artifacts, including earspools, panpipes, effigy figurines, engraved copper gorgets, head plates and headdresses, bone hair pins, silver and copper tablets, game stones, greenstone axes, flint blades, and zoomorphic effigy vessels (to list just a few), they have really only added to the mystery and intrigue surrounding the "Mound Builders" as these ancient peoples are now known. These standing testaments to early man's extraordinary accomplishments continue to speak of a period of time about which scholars can only theorize. With no evidence of a written language and a high probability that associated groups spoke different languages (based on the earliest lingual patterns encountered from each region), what the so-called "Mound Builders" accomplished in the span of a few centuries is nothing short of phenomenal.

Native American Tribes: The History and Culture of the Mound Builders comprehensively covers the facts, mysteries, and theories surrounding the ancient Native Americans who built the elaborate mounds, discussing what is known and unknown about their origins. Along with pictures and a bibliography, you will learn about the Mound Builders like you never have before, in no time at all.

Effigy pot found at the Nodena Site in present-day Arkansas

Chapter 1: Discovering the Mound Builders

The mound of the Great Sun in Grand Village of the Natchez (Mississippi) was built around 1200 A.D.

One of the first things the European settlers noticed in North America was the seemingly countless numbers of very large mounds built across the landscape of the continent, and naturally that gave rise to several early theories. When conquistador Hernando de Soto made a trek through the southeastern part of North America from 1540-42, his expedition came across natives who had fortified towns with these mounds, which the Spaniards figured were probably their version of a temple. De Soto also came across one group still building new mounds, and their queen, a woman named Cofitachequi, explained to him that the mounds were burial grounds for the elite members of the natives' society. Similarly, French artist Jacques Le Moyne came across another society in present-day northeastern Florida and drew a rendition of a chief's burial, writing the caption, "Sometimes the deceased king of this province is buried with great solemnity..."

In the 1750s, French Jesuits made their way down the Mississippi River and made contact with a native tribe now known as the Natchez in Mississippi. The explorers found a giant settlement spread out across several villages, and the high chief had his residence built atop the largest mound. Maturin Le Petit, a Jesuit priest, recorded that the chief came out of his residence atop the mound each morning and "greeted the rising sun, invoking thanks and blowing tobacco smoke to the four cardinal directions."

In the English colonies to the north and east, mounds were also found, and in 1787, American botanist, naturalist, and physician Benjamin S. Barton addressed the Mound Builder phenomenon in his *Observations on Some Parts of Natural History*, incorrectly attributing the prehistoric mounds of Ohio to the Danes. He later withdrew that theory in what would be recognized as the first scholarly treatise published on the subject, his *New Views of the Origin of the Tribes and Nations of America*, in which he identifies the Mound Builders as "Native Americans of a higher cultural level." Soon after Barton's work was published, renowned scholar and Harvard librarian Reverend Thaddeus M. Harris of Massachusetts expressed his belief that the Mound Builders were a "civilization," a word not commonly applied to any Native American groups of the time.

Around 1812, American historian Dr. James H. McColloh began a study of the Mound Builders, publishing *Researches in America* in 1816, which he would revise numerous times over a 12-year period as new understandings arose. One of the first to surmise that the Ohio Mound Builders originated in the South, McColloh stated that Native Americans were the ones who created the mounds, a theory he based on skull similarity (which, while supported by other scholars of the day, lacked scientific evidence). Finally resigning himself to the highly speculative nature of his conclusions, he wrote,:

"When we contemplate the ruins of Illium, or Carthage, or of Palmyra, amid all our regret and concern for their fate, yet there are incidents connected with their histories which we reflect on with enthusiasm. Though they have fallen, their fame yet lives. But with the mounds and fortifications of America, we have no agreeable, no inspiring associations. We see 'The bones of men in some forgotten battle slain'--we see the labours of their hands desolated--their rude works overgrown by the trees of the forest-- whilst the nation that raised these works, together with her patriots and her heroes, had disappeared, and has not left even a name behind . . . Until very lately, it was believed, that the Indians in the neighbourhood of these remains, were entirely ignorant of the erectors of these works--and which they almost universally referred to an age anteriour to their earliest traditions. Fortunately, however, some gentlemen of curiosity have attended to this subject--scarcely in time; but who have preserved some traditions which throw a light upon the dark inquiry; -- and by means of which, we may be able to piece the mysteries which shroud other, and equally interesting subjects."[1]

---

[1] McCulloh, James H., M.D. An Attempt to Settle Some Points Relative to the Aborigines of America. *Pages 209—210.*

Even decades later, when numerous world-renowned academics and adventurers had published their views concerning the mysterious earthworks and the true identity of the "Mound Builders", different theories continued to be put out. One of the most popular contentions was that the mounds were probably built by migrating Mexicans, while other theories sited ancient Vikings or wandering Hindus as the architects. Just before running for the presidency in 1840, William Henry Harrison offered the theory that the Aztec civilization rose from the Midwestern Mound Builders, hypothesizing that since the Mound Builders seemed to have disappeared in the early 8th century and the Aztecs rose about the same time, the two civilizations must be related.

Another theory that seemed reasonable to academics and novices alike was that the mounds were constructed by a Lost Tribe of Israel, a theory promoted by prolific author and famed scholar Noah Webster. Even in modern times, many Ojibway Native Americans trace their culture to the Lost Tribes, with Ojibway scholar William W. Warren writing, "they are either descendants of the lost tribes of Israel, or they had, in some former era, a close contact and intercourse with the Hebrews, imbibing from them their beliefs and customs and the traditions of their patriarchs"[2]

In many scholars' minds, there is little doubt that the Mound Builders were a pious people whose society was founded on spiritual beliefs and religious adherence on a massive scale. Indeed, most Mound Builder earthworks scattered across North America are burial sites where elaborate ritual is evident.

Chapter 2: The Adena

While archaeologists can only speculate as to who first walked the vast expanses of the North American continent, evidence of Paleoindian (first culture) activity -- particularly that of the Clovis and Folsom peoples -- can be traced back at least 12,000 years through the archaeological fossil record. Radiocarbon dating estimates the Clovis, the earlier of the two, occupied North America between 11,050 B.C. and 10,800 B.C. Although pre-Clovis finds indicate human occupation of North America as early as 13,000 B.C., with the earliest occupation speculated to be as early as 50,000 B.C., most physical evidence was erased from the landscape by glacial movement during the Ice Age.

These first post-Ice Age inhabitants were undoubtedly hunter-gatherers who used stone and bone tools to utilize the seemingly limitless bounty of wild resources they discovered, but virtually nothing is known about their social or organizational habits. In fact, most theories concerning their place in pre-history are based strictly on the distinctive "fluted-base" stone points they used in hunting.

Beginning about 8900 B.C. the archaeological record suggests a succession of people settled,

---

[2] Warren, William W. *History of the Ojibway People.* Page 63.

flourished, and then faded from the Ohio River Valley, the area extending through the North American states of Pennsylvania, Ohio, West Virginia, Kentucky, Indiana, and Illinois. Most likely drawn to the diverse array of vegetation, terrain, water sources, and wild game this area offers in abundance, numerous rock shelters, hunting camps, flint-knapping sites, agricultural hamlets, and mound-oriented ceremonial centers attest to their prolonged occupation of many areas.

Slowly evolving from a big-game hunting economy into one based on foraging and smaller game, a dynamic culture of the so-called "Mound Builder Tradition" emerged from the upper Ohio River Valley about 700 B.C., known as the Adena. Though not the first to build mounds in North America, an achievement credited to the Watson Brake Mound Complex Culture in Ouachita Parish, Louisiana, around 3500 B.C., the Adena, who were actually dozens of local cultures living as cooperative and interactive neighbors, built earthworks much more impressive in design than their neighbors to the southwest. Most importantly from the sociological perspective, the Adena are believed to have been the first to develop communities centered around such works, where formal communal rituals and burial ceremonies were practiced.

Early 20th century picture of the Adena Mound near present-day Chillicothe, Ohio

An Adena Mound built near present-day Miamisburg, Ohio

Initially settling into scattered "hamlets" of 10-12 families near streams or rivers where the rich bottomland could produce enough vegetation to accommodate a sedentary lifestyle, the early Adena spent their days like most indigenous peoples of the period: hunting, gathering, exploring their resource options, and meeting daily needs. Flora remains from various Adena sites support the likelihood that they were among the first to incorporate cultivated plant foods into their diets, growing maygrass, sump weed, sunflower for their edible seeds, and perhaps squash, all as early as 600 B.C.

Within just a few centuries, the Adena developed a social structure far more complex than any indigenous group of North America had before, coming to virtually dominate the Eastern landscape from Indiana's Whitewater River Valley in the west to Pittsburgh in the upper Ohio River Valley in the east. It also stretched from the Blue Grass of central Kentucky north to the upper reaches of the Acioto and Muskingum rivers of Ohio, and Adena mounds and artifacts have been found as far north as the Canadian Maritimes and Mid-Atlantic states.

Thought to have begun with the burial of a single individual, perhaps a village leader, shaman, or the child of a prominent member of society, formal Adena mound building practices most likely developed with the formation of a "mortuary cult," a cleric-like order that began adding "capping" layers of earth with each subsequent burial. Over time, this would form a larger mound of communal significance, where acts of reverence were routinely demonstrated. As the Adena sociocultural structure became increasingly more ritualized, the hamlets' residents cooperated in ongoing construction of additional mortuary centers; centers which over time took on the distinctive cone-shaped mound design the Adena are noted for today, a design that differentiates them from their successors, the Hopewell. Scholars believe settlements like those at Marietta represent sites initially chosen by the Adena for one specific purpose: to bury the dead in accordance with their evolving spiritual beliefs. Some believe the Adena chose geographic locations with prior spiritual significance.

Initially, individual interment methods varied, depending upon the ritual practices in place at that time, and funerary customs varied greatly from being simple to more complex. Burial chambers were sometimes lined with bark or logs, creating tomb-like roofed structures, and many of the dead were found covered in red ocher or accompanied by large chunks of ochre placed beside them in the grave, reflective of burial practices dating back to the Neanderthal in "Neander's Valley," Germany circa 70,000 B.C. Thin slabs of deeply grooved limestone and sandstone have also been recovered, believed to have been used as tablets to prepare ochre and graphite into a paint that may have been applied to the corpses.

Some interments contained intact bodies, others consisted of cremated remains, and it appears that in some cases mourners simply deposited bundles of bones as if the body had been exposed to the elements until the flesh decayed. It is also possible that the bones had been retrieved from distant locations and brought back for reburial. At Cresap Mound in West Virginia, the skull of the deceased was placed on the lap and bore a slightly *polished* look, as if it had been handled regularly for quite some time prior to interment. Physical orientation also seems to have factored into some grave sites, with some bodies placed in an intentional east-west orientation, suggesting cardinal point observance or astronomical alignment.

As Adena ceremonialism grew more complex and mortuary cults grew more influential, pieces of flint, copper bracelets and breastplates, finger rings, stone tablets, marine shell beads, cut mica, stone effigy pipes (usually resembling birds, fish, or even a full human figure), and pieces of broken pottery were routinely buried with the dead. And in the final period of Adena cultural development during the 1st century B.C., some corpses were first placed in wooden funerary buildings called "charnel houses," which, after a number of bodies had been accumulated, were ritually burned. Meanwhile, other bodies were cremated in circular or elliptical clay basins dug into the earth, reflecting an apparent evolution of mortuary practices and beliefs.

Other further developed sites included circular earthen enclosures consisting of shallow ditches and adjacent embankments near the burial mounds, which anthropologists refer to as "sacred circles". These sacred circles are believed to have been meeting places for kin groups using the same associated mound. At other sites, this concept appears to have been developed even further, with multiple sacred circles occurring in groups of two to eight, where people from different social units could congregate, perhaps for some specialized or less-localized communal ritual.

Judging by the incredible array of exotic grave goods found at Adena sites that would have been foreign to their geographic location, their evolving spirituality fueled their societal expansion and organization, and over time it prompted the construction of more substantial homes, expanded utilization of pottery, and increased manipulation of their surroundings. Over a period of perhaps 200 years, the Adena managed to both establish a stable means by which to meet their cultures' ever-expanding spiritual obligations and a far-reaching trade network to bring in foodstuffs not locally grown. The trade apparently consisted of an extensive exchange system by which copper from the north, shells and feathers from the south, and various ritual goods like grizzly bear teeth from the west (which were used in ever-more elaborate funerary ceremonies) could be acquired. Some items were made of Lake Superior copper, *kinnikinnick* pipes from Ohio were traded to Adena sites in Maryland, New England, and Ontario. Effigy stones from Wisconsin also attest to this far-flung exchange.

Even more significantly, the Adena may also have been the first people of North America to establish the concept of spiritual pilgrimages, a concept thought to have been an essential element of the "Hopewell Tradition". Given the extent of At their peak of cultural influence, the Adena occupied a significant portion of the middle Ohio River Valley and thousands of square miles in all directions--a remarkable achievement for any people of any period. But as extensive and well-established as the Adena culture appears to have been, it would prove mere groundwork lain for the extraordinary culture that would come to dominate the Woodland regions by 150 B.C.. Indeed, as mortuary practices even more elaborate than their own began to emerge from their neighbors the Hopewell, the Adena slowly faded into the cultural landscape--their accomplishments usurped and absorbed by this next great society. Beyond a doubt, North America had never seen anything with the power and magnitude of the "Hopewell Tradition"—nor is likely to see again.

Chapter 3: The Hopewell

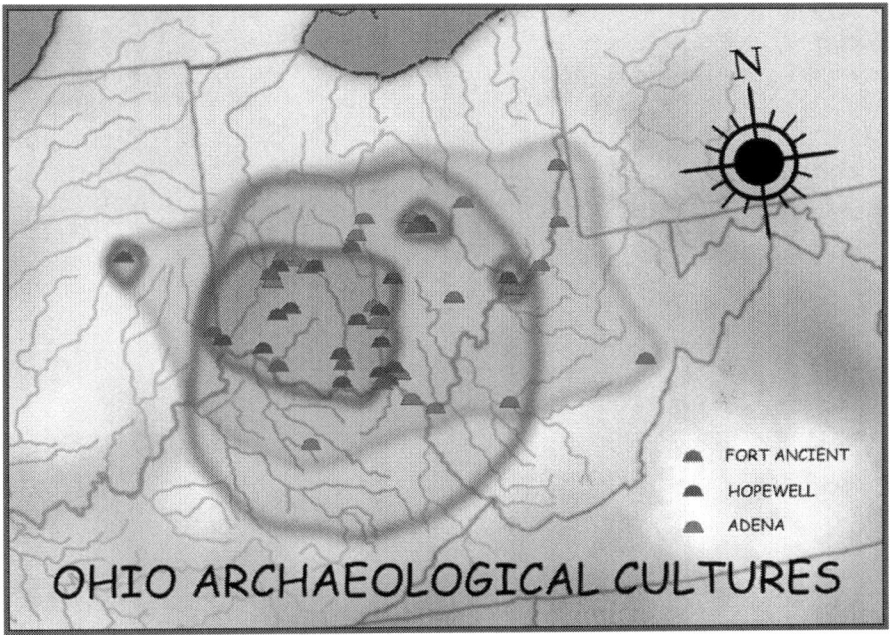

The location of Hopewell and Adena sites in Ohio

First referenced in 1820 by American archaeologist Caleb Atwater (1778--1867), the so-called "Hopewell Tradition" (often incorrectly referred to as the "Hopewell culture") is most commonly associated with the extraordinary burial mounds and geometric earthwork complexes that various socially-related populations constructed throughout Ohio (at places like Newark, Fort Ancient, and Mound City) and thousands of other sites across North America. One Hopewell site reached as far south as Tampa Bay, Florida.

Thought to have originated in western New York or western Illinois, the Ohio Hopewell have been fascinating archaeologists for nearly two centuries. Over that time, a number of mounds have been measured and mapped, producing an amazing cache of artifacts that includes clay altars, sculptured sandstone tablets, bone carvings, celt-shaped polished limestone, bone awls, plates of mica, headdresses, copper plates and ornaments, and tens of thousands of other cultural items. Named for the farmer who owned the site at Chillicothe in south-central Ohio where the first official archaeological investigation took place in the 1880's, the Hopewell Mound Group's "type site" designation (meaning a site displaying features *typifying* a given culture) was subsequently applied to the entire tradition.

   Now recognized as a far-reaching interactive network of related cultural *traditions* rather than a single unified society, the Hopewell Tradition reflects common artifact style, architecture, and, presumably, mortuary beliefs. Instead of comprising a single "tribe" with villages spread across the countryside, anthropologists today acknowledge the Kansas City Hopewell, Marksville Hopewell (of the lower Mississippi Valley), Swift Creek Hopewell (of Georgia, Alabama, Florida, South Carolina, and Tennessee), Copena Hopewell (of northern Alabama, Mississippi, Tennessee, and Kentucky), and Havana Hopewell (of Iowa, Illinois, and Missouri), as well as a number of other Hopewellian-like societies found throughout the eastern and southern regions of North America, as distinguishable adherents of the "tradition." By extension, a dozen more indigenous groups based as far south as central Florida, including the Manasota of Tampa Bay are also included.

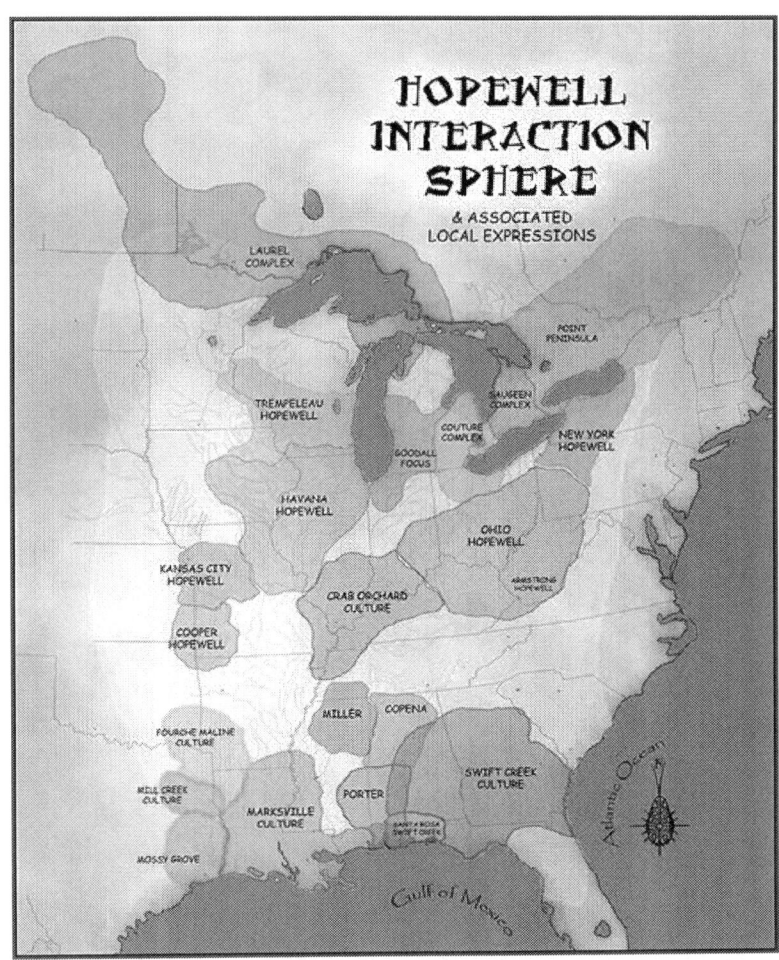

The Hopewell Interaction Sphere

Central to understanding the societal and apparent spiritual underpinnings of the Hopewell Tradition is, of course, the extraordinary earthworks built between 200 B.C. and 500 A.D. Although mounds of earth or stone had become common landscape features across the East and Midwest a century before, due partially to the Adena, the majority of those were circular or oval-shaped piles of earth rarely more than a few yards high, with the biggest being the elongated types built over mortuary structures like those found at Newark in central Ohio. Soon after the

Hopewell appeared on the cultural landscape, however, more and more elaborate earthwork designs began to appear, with three major building styles quickly diverging: embankment earthworks, mounds covering ritually "prepared" floors, and timber constructions, the majority of which were later destroyed and covered by more substantial earthen works. Several of the most impressive Ohio sites include all three types, some with spectacular earthen walls connecting them.

Mound City Hopewell site near Chillicothe, Ohio.

Major Hopewellian mounds were usually constructed in layers of specially-selected earths, clays, stones, and gravels that were often transported considerable distances. Timber structures were capped with what anthropologists call "prepared" floors of gravel and clay, before subsequent layers were added. While not all Hopewellian earthworks included mounds, those that did often utilized crematory basins, "prepared" burial platforms, and crypts, with the majority containing human remains accompanied by exotic and local grave goods. And despite the fact many of these mounds appear superficially similar, they are actually quite different internally, as individual graves were constructed in a variety of methods with varying numbers of individuals entombed.

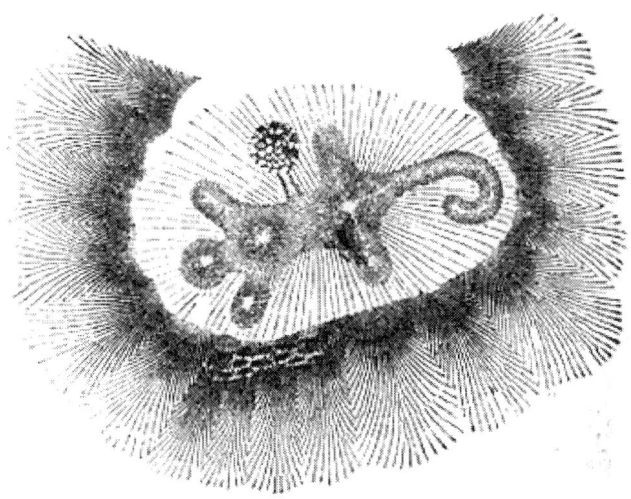

This illustration depicts the layout of the "Alligator Effigy Mound", constructed in Ohio around 950 A.D.

Although many scholars agree that these amazing monuments were most likely centers of ceremony, and quite significant if not essential to societal organization, it is still not entirely clear what significance they held for the Hopewell people, or why they varied so greatly in style and structure. As seen at sites along the Great Miami, Little Miami, and Scioto rivers, the Hopewell used a wide range of mortuary methods, perhaps based on the social role of the individual or individuals entombed. Judging from the ritual behavior of modern-day societies, it is quite likely that those included in the mound funerary system were clan or lineage leaders honored in death with special funeral ceremonies and specially-chosen artifacts. In many cases, their burial sites were adorned with ceremonial items that acknowledged their importance within their given group. Whether their importance was personal, spiritual, political, military, or economic is impossible to determine.

In any regard, the rituals associated with mound interment likely not only commemorated an individual of particular societal status but also served to further validate group identity. Those honored in this way were most likely key figures who contributed to organizing community efforts to erect burial mounds, construct earthworks, and carry out other communally-beneficial projects. As renowned archaeologist Dr. David S. Brose of University of Michigan explains, "Such mechanisms provided increasing social and economic stability, reinforced trends towards sedentary living and specialized exploitation of local resources, and probably led to population growth."[3]

At Hopewell City, for example, each of the 24 mounds was built over a "charnel house," with significant evidence of widespread "aggrandizing" reflected in the inclusion of great quantities of highly-prized copper, obsidian, and mica grave goods. This probably indicated high societal position or prominence. Furthermore, some of the mounds included "trophy skulls" and hundreds of elegant, locally-crafted stone smoking pipes, indicating both a long-distance exotic trade and a large-scale local production. Most historians believe Hopewellian "trophy skulls" were the remains of honored relatives rather than defeated enemies, a tradition perhaps dating to the Adena.

Furthermore, the Hopewellians are believed to have practiced reciprocation, with most of the deceased's food and other worldly possessions being redistributed amongst all those participating in the burial ceremony. Thus, when prized "high-status" goods like mica sheets, copper ornaments, and carved smoking pipes were buried with their owners, it not only proclaimed that individual's special societal status but maintained their prestige for posterity by having their best items vanishing below the ground for eternity.

However, at the Newark site, of the 16 known mounds, only 6 contained burials. Moreover, "trophy skulls" were conspicuously absent, and no mounds approach the monumental size of those at Hopewell. Perhaps most significantly, the majority of burials at Newark were interred in a large communal burial area with few grave goods included, exotic or otherwise. Thus, while Hopewellian mortuary practices were obviously highly ceremonial, there appears to have been no "all-encompassing" tenets regarding the method. And despite all the apparent pageantry surrounding death, and the long-held belief that the Hopewell maintained a stratified society or perhaps even a caste system, there is no evidence of special treatment being afforded individuals during their lifetimes, regardless of which burial model was in practice at the time. In fact, in most cases it's impossible to distinguish between the burials of the prominent and those of the commoner without looking inside their tombs. To explain this, some scholars speculate that certain Hopewellian societies included an artisan community whose specific job was to replenish and regularly replace grave goods.

While many historians of the past were quick to connect the proverbial dots between the thousands of mounds across the continent and arrive at a map showing a cohesive, unified society – a civilization or empire, in essence -- for every argument supporting interregional organization, there are two opposing it. Archaeologist David Brose contends that while sociocultural growth triggered better-integrated social systems that replaced more flexible ones of earlier times, there was most likely a "trajectory" of long-term cultural exchange. Brose explained, "The more closely integrated social systems [of the Hopewellian Tradition] emphasized rank within individual lineages, validated by exotic objects of great prestige from afar and by seasonal ceremonies when all the members of lineages, from near and far, came

---

[3] Fagan, Brian. *The First North Americans: An Archaeological Journey*. Page 208.

together to reinforce social identity and common goals."[4] These goals, however, were not universal across the so-called Hopewellian "sphere", and they varied in importance from population to population.

Even with tens of thousands of artifacts to tell the tale, the best scholars can offer today is a patchwork picture-puzzle of a seemingly complex society whose socioreligious ideology so impressed neighboring groups that it became the prevailing model of societal development throughout the entire eastern half of North America. At the same time, each Hopewellian society varied so greatly from site to site and city to city that no single site can be regarded as the model of the "Hopewellian Tradition." In fact, while some sites appear to suggest a well-balanced economy based on hunting, fishing, and agriculture encompassed by minimal ritual adherence, others appear to have been strictly oriented towards hunting and gathering, perhaps to devote more time to ritual involvement. Others seemingly had an artisan sector committed to crafting the exquisite tools, weapons, textiles, and ornamental objects typically buried with the dead.

Chronologically-speaking, the Adena and Hopewell occupy a period of North American prehistory referred to in anthropological circles as the "Early Woodland" and "Middle Woodland" periods respectively. While "Woodland" is often used to indicate the advent of specific cultural developments not previously appearing in the archaeological fossil record, it is the widespread use of pottery and ceramics that categorically demarcates the onset of the Early Woodland Period and separates it from the Archaic Period at roughly 1000 B.C.. The emergence of Hopewellian ceremonial practices marked the commencement of the Middle Woodland Period at roughly 150 B.C. While these dates can and do vary from source to source, it is generally accepted that the Adena occupied the Ohio River Valley from approximately 700 B.C. to 200 A.D., with the Hopewell occupation from approximately 400 B.C. to 600 A.D. Given that there was an obvious period of co-existence between the two, differentiating and distinguishing the two cultural traditions from each other has been a point of contention among anthropologists for more than a century, with some contending that the Hopewell Tradition was actually an Adena offshoot.

Concurrent with recognized Hopewellian ceremonial practices were a number of other cultural innovations now closely associated with the Middle Woodland Period, including stone and bone tool-crafting, leather working, cloth production, plant cultivation, shelter construction, and, of course, more complex methods of mound building. These associated traits are particularly relevant to Hopewellian scholars due to the fact that they are not initially found in the southeastern part of the country (in present-day South Carolina and points further south), despite the fact they first appeared in an area extending from the upper Mississippi River Valley to southern New England around 1000 B.C. In fact, it would seemingly be another 2,000 years before these ideas and practices spread to other areas of North America, prompting more than a

---

[4] Fagan, Brian. *The First North Americans: An Archaeological Journey*. Page 208.

few scholars to question why.

For example, the earliest known pottery of the northern regions is a "grit-tempered" (crushed granite) cord or plain type clay pot made with a simple *subconoidal* (rounded cone or ovoid shape) base. These have a much different geographic origin than earlier "Gulf Formational" ceramics found in the southeast that date back from 2000 B.C. to the 1st century A.D. Through the apparent trade of ceramics between northern groups (presumably the Adena and Hopewell) and southern indigenous groups, southern pottery, most notably the "Deptford" (quartz sand-tempered) pottery of the Georgian-South Carolina region used to demarcate the onset of the Woodland Period, began taking on northern characteristics, with an obvious blending of ceramic modes between these two once distinctly-different pottery styles. This sociocultural phenomenon is further emphasized in areas of the southeast where northern interaction was limited and Gulf Coast ceramics remained virtually unchanged. Apparent by the preponderance of Hopewellian pottery and mortuary goods found at various settlements across the southeast by Middle Woodland times, not only did the Hopewellian Tradition influence numerous societies of this region, it appears to have virtually replaced regional traditions of earlier periods in some places.

The archaeological record suggests that Hopewellian ceremonialism reached the southeast early in the 1st century A.D., presumably via far-reaching trade. And while the cultural origin of mound building in central and northeastern North America is still open to debate, there is little doubt that burial mounds of the Southeast evolved directly from the Hopewell Tradition, with three easily discernible periods reflecting specific cultural diffusion mirroring known Hopewellian development: the Southeastern Burial Mound 1 Period (1st century A.D. to 300 A.D.), Southeastern Burial Mound 2 Period (300-600 A.D.), and Southeastern Burial Mound 3 Period (600-1000 A.D.

As can still be seen throughout South Carolina, Alabama, and Georgia today, mounds of the "Mound 1" Period exhibit strong similarities to Ohio Hopewell structures, most of which contain grave goods (copper panpipes, earspools, anthropomorphic figures, platform pipes, and exotic pottery) of Hopewellian design. During the "Mound 2" Period, southeastern mortuary rites evolved into a variety of diverse regional styles that varied from group to group, with some groups even opting for caves rather than mounds and locally-crafted grave goods instead of foreign ones. These cultural developments directly correspond with the apparent decline of the Hopewellian trade system, which in turn spurred regional differentiation as northern wares became increasingly more difficult to acquire. While some copper earspools, reel-shaped gorgets, and galena (a crystalline mineral) were still used, there was a noticeable increase in Gulf Coast cups and shells, evidence of an intensified southerly trade shift.

True to this developmental pattern, the "Mound 3" Period reflects post-Hopewellian evolution, characterized by a cessation of mound building over much of North America, a sharp decrease in the exchange of exotic goods (perhaps indicative of a total trade-system collapse), the advance of regional specialization that was nevertheless clearly founded on traditional Hopewellian motifs, and the rise of the Weeden Island culture along the Florida Gulf coast. This period is characterized by small conical earthen mounds, usually containing the remains of relatively fewer individuals. The mounds often hold less than a dozen bodies, perhaps members of a single family or clan, and marine shell cups and ornaments were the only traditional long-distance trade goods still exchanged (though local copper ornaments and elbow ceremonial pipes are sometimes present). Thus, even though the Hopewellian "sphere" extended throughout the southeast, their direct influence waned in the region at the same time their culture was waning elsewhere.

Chapter 4: Other Significant Mound Building Cultures

After the spread of the Hopewellian Tradition and advancement of Hopewellian ritualism, the ultimate disintegration of Hopewellian influence left a vacuum to be filled by new cultures, and a number of other significant "mound building" cultures apparently popped up throughout the eastern part of the continent.

Troyville-Coles Creek Culture

Considered by some scholars to have been part of the "Mississippian" Tradition, and considered by others to be a predecessor of it, the Troyville-Coles Creek Culture was a Late Woodland mound building offshoot of the Hopewellian Tradition that flourished in the Lower Mississippi River Valley from approximately 800-1500 A.D.

This culture ultimately instigated a significant change in the sociocultural direction of the region. Though established prior to the rise of corn/maize-oriented "chiefdom" societies, by 1000 A.D. the Troyville-Coles Creek Culture had instituted sociopolitical polices based on a class of social elites, with sociopolitical complexity significantly increased by the end of the Troyville-Coles Creek period. With Troyville-Coles Creek sites found in Arkansas, Louisiana, Oklahoma, Mississippi, and Texas, this tradition is often considered ancestral to the Plaquemine Culture (which lasted from 1000-1600 A.D.).

Mississippian Tradition

From 900-1450 A.D., the Mississippian Tradition developed, spread, and diversified across the eastern part of the continent, primarily along the river valleys. While the term "Mississippian" defies specific definition, what sets it apart from other North American cultural traditions are their social and religious institutions, which were defined by their highly-distinctive sacred artifacts. These reflected a triad of religious cults based on warfare, fertility, and ancestor worship, and they apparently lay at the core of Mississippian society.

Known from an array of exotic motifs and symbols and the use of highly-valued raw materials like copper and sea shells, the Mississippian Warfare Cult was apparently an important power-base for the elite class of the Mississippian Tradition. In addition to war axes, maces, and a variety of other deadly weapons, *elite* burial artifacts included peculiar cosmic imagery. Animals, humans, and mythic beasts appear to reference legendary warrior-heroes in the act of supernatural feats, and artifacts were stored in sacred bundles kept by priests that meld warfare, cosmology, and nobility into one cohesive unit. Though the Mississippian influence is not believed to have been as culturally interconnected as that of the Hopewell, features of their War-Cult motifs have been seen as far east as Alabama and Georgia, and as far west as Spiro, Oklahoma.

The Mississippian Earth/Fertility Cult was likely the most direct link to the Hopewellian Tradition, reflected in the flat-topped earthen platform mounds characteristic of their many centers. Thought to represent the Southeast Native American belief that the earth is a flat surface oriented toward four quarters of the world, the mounds apparently acted as monumental symbols of renewal and fertility, with the platform feature representing the earth. There are historically-documented connections between the mounds and the communal "green corn" ceremony witnessed by early Europeans that celebrated the new harvest and the fertility of the earth, versions of which survived into modern times.

Ancestor Cults, of which there appears to have been multiple, were apparently a very powerful element of Mississippian society that provided a vital connection between the living and the (ancestral) land. It's believed the most prominent site for these cults was the Great Mortuary in the Craig Mound, which was built on the site of several funerary structures (perhaps charnel houses). The Mortuary contained clumps of human bones and artifacts proven to have been retrieved from other sites, and these clumps were then laid on a floor made of cane. Formal burials were interred above them, accompanied by baskets of ceremonial objects such as copper-headed axes, textiles, containers of sea shells, wooden masks, and statues. Everything was then ceremoniously sealed.

The Craig Mound

Each Mississippian cult was separate and distinct. Priests were thought to possess supernatural powers, and warriors held different chiefly roles, but both groups were confined to their respective kin groups, a social structure that was similar to those found in various Native American tribes across North America when the Europeans arrived. Through elaborate ceremonies, political power was validated, with Fertility Cults emphasizing communal rites involving entire kin groups and priests maintaining the temples, burial houses, and sacred fires. Ancestor worship encompassed all sectors of Mississippian society, and with priests in a powerful position to mediate disputes and competing cult interests. Mississippian specialist Dr. James Knight, of the University of Alabama's Department of Anthropology, writes, " . . . these powerful cults, which defined both chiefly and communal society, transcended the South and Southeast and all their different cultural and ecological boundaries. They created a dynamic, constantly changing and highly factionalized society with tremendous variation in social complexity. Large centers like Cahokia, near St. Louis, lay at one end of this spectrum of complexity, hundreds of small centers and minor chiefdoms at the other."[5]

The largest and most influential urban settlement of Mississippian development, Cahokia, was located in southern Illinois, directly across the Mississippi River from what would become East Saint Louis. A huge metropolis some five to six square miles in area, Cahokia contained

---

[5] Fagan, Brian. *The First North Americans: An Archaeological Journey.* Page 223.

hundreds of mounds grouped around central plazas and is believed to have supported a population estimated at 10,000-30,000 at its peak (around 1250 A.D.). If so, this city was as large as or larger than any European city of the time, and a population that size would not be surpassed by any city in the United States until nearly 1800. Assumed to have been settled around 600 A.D. during the Late Woodland Period, with mound building beginning about 800 A.D., the site may have originally contained an estimated 120 earthen mounds, and 80 remain today.

Some of the Cahokia Mounds

The largest structure at Cahokia was a massive platform mound 10 stories in height with four terraces. Known as Monk's Mound, it is the largest man-made earthen mound north of Mexico. Developed over the course of several centuries, through at least 10 separate construction periods, Monks Mound was aptly named for the community of Trappist monks that resided there for a short time after European settlement. Excavation of the peak of the Mound has revealed evidence of a 5000-square-foot building (105 feet long x 48 feet wide x 50 feet high), presumably a temple or residence of the supreme chief that could have been seen from virtually any place in the city. In July 1964, Cahokia was designated a National Historic Landmark, the only such designation in Illinois.

(Note: Not all anthropologists attribute Cahokia specifically to the Mississippian Tradition. Some credit an earlier culture with its founding.)

Fort Ancient Culture

From 1000-1670 A.D., the Fort Ancient Mound Building Culture evolved from the

Mississippian Tradition and came to dominate a large portion of southern Ohio, northern Kentucky, and western West Virginia. However, it apparently had few ties with the various Hopewellian-styled societies evolving to the south during the same time.

Having developed distinctive cultural habits that distinguished them from other Mississippian or Hopewellian groups, Fort Ancient sites indicate a greater dependency on corn (maize) and native cultigens, less of a hierarchical social structure than neighboring groups, the trademark construction of stockades (lending to their "fort" designation), and the adoption of funerary practices by 1500 A.D. These practices consisted of interring the dead in coffin-like stone boxes in graves often located within the villages. Studies of Fort Ancient grave goods, which were comparatively limited, suggest a "tribal confederacy" rather than the "chiefdom" structure of Mississippian cultures to the west, and by some reckoning, the modern-day Shawnee may be descendants of Fort Ancient. Among their greatest achievement is the mysterious "Great Serpent Mound" of Ohio.

The Great Serpent Mound in Ohio is the largest effigy mound in North America

Though long erroneously attributed to the Adena Culture, due to nearby conical mounds characteristic of the Adena, the Great Serpent Mound, located on a plateau of the Serpent Mound Crater along Ohio Brush Creek in Adams County, Ohio, has since been radiocarbon-dated to the

Fort Ancient Culture period. Believed to have been constructed about 1070 A.D., this 1,348-foot-long, three-foot-high prehistoric serpentine effigy mound (which has no mortuary purpose) resembles an uncoiling snake about to swallow an egg. However, a number of other theories persist regarding its origins, including the suggestion that the serpent is actually a model of the Little Dipper constellation with its tail coiled around the North Star. The longest known serpentine effigy mound in the world, the Serpent Mound is embedded with cave-like, hollow structures that have led archaeologists to speculate that there may be more of the mysterious land feature buried underground, either by design or as a result of shifting terrain.

Plaquemine Culture

Believed to have been an offshoot of the Troyville-Coles Creek Mississippian Culture, the Plaquemine Culture flourished throughout Louisiana (except in the northwest, where the Caddo were established) and the lower Mississippi River Valley. In keeping with patterns established by their ancestors, the Plaquemine built large ceremonial centers with two or more large flat-topped pyramidal mounds facing an open central plaza. Constructed in several stages, with some eventually measuring more than 100 feet on a side and 10 feet high, some mounds were crowned with one or two smaller mounds. Often constructed on the ruins of an older house or temple, circular buildings of wattle and daub were constructed, sometimes with wall posts sunk into foot-deep wall trenches. In some cases, the Plaquemine dug shallow oval or rectangular graves in the mounds as well. While these may have been for primary burials, it appears that in many cases they were for the reburial of remains retrieved from elsewhere, which might have been part of a ritualized process. Remarkably, some graves contained only skulls, with one of the graves containing 66 skulls, and grave goods included pottery, pipes, stone points, and axes made of ground stone. Examples of their earthworks are found at the Medora Site in West Baton Rouge Parish, Louisiana, the Anna, Emerald Mound in Winterville, and Holly Bluff (Lake George) sites in Mississippi. Some anthropologists believe the Plaquemine Culture are ancestral to the Natchez and Taensa peoples, members of which survive in modern-day Oklahoma.

The Emerald Mound Site

Marksville Culture

Sharing many Hopewellian mortuary customs, as well as ritual and religious beliefs and artifact styles, the Marksville Culture (named for the Marksville Prehistoric Indian Site in Marksville, Louisiana) became a regional force along the Lower Mississippi Valley, Yazoo Valley, and Tensas Valley areas of Louisiana, Mississippi, Missouri, and Arkansas from approximately 100 B.C. to 400 A.D. A southern arm of the Hopewellian network, Marksville settlements were large and usually located on terraces of major streams, with burial mounds thought to have been constructed for individuals of high (perhaps hierarchical) social status. They contained exotic grave goods such as copper panpipes, earspools, bracelets and beads, rare minerals, stone platform pipes, mica figurines (typical of Hopewellian burials), marine shells, freshwater pearls, and greenstone celts. Some scholars believe the Marksville Culture evolved into the Troyville-Coles Creek and Plum Bayou cultures.

Swift Creek Culture

More accurately termed a "tradition" than a "culture" (although many scholars contend that the Swift Creek were a single group), the Swift Creek Tradition grew around 100 A.D., spreading across the Tennessee, Georgia, South Carolina, and north Florida landscape, where it flourished until about 800 A.D. Although the Swift Creek erected multiple Hopewellian-styled mound centers, exemplified by the Kolomoki site located at Kolomoki Mounds State Park in Blakely, Georgia, it is their distinctive pottery type by which they are most commonly identified. This pottery was apparently traded as far north as Ohio, suggesting that the trade of the pottery was what their economy was also based on. Known as "Swift Creek Complicated Stamped," their pottery is noted for its distinctive decoration and complex curvilinear pattern, a design carved into a wooden paddle used to "stamp" the soft clay before it was fired.

Copena Culture

Today the Copena Culture, whose name was derived from the first three letters of *copper* and the last three letters of the mineral galena, is most closely associated with the Copena Mortuary Complex of the Tennessee River Valley in northern Alabama, where some 50 relatively-elaborate burial mounds constructed over subsoil burial pits were discovered. Closely reflecting the Hopewellian Tradition model, the Copena Culture, who by some calculations became a prominent force across the southeast as early as 2000 B.C. and endured to 800 A.D., lined their burial pits with clay, log or bark, with interred bodies placed on bark matting. These burial sites have provided great insight into regional ceremonial practices via the selection of copper reel-shaped gorgets, earspools, bracelets, celts, beads, marine shell cups, and elbow ritual pipes recovered in abundance. They also provide insight into the elaborate trade network thought to have been established by the Hopewell that was centered in Ohio.

Crab Orchard Tradition

The Crab Orchard Tradition is a cultural group believed to have occupied a region that was virtually surrounded by competing Hopewellian groups, with Copina and Miller groups to the south, Ohio Hopewell to the east, and Havana, Kansas City, and Cooper Hopewellian groups to the west). Nevertheless, the Crab Orchard Tradition grew from a small and widely dispersed population into a regional force concentrated on the terrace and floodplains of the Ohio River in southern Indiana, southern Illinois, and particularly western Kentucky. Though most identified by their particular variety of pottery, a fabric-impressed ware valued for its distinctive finish, their large "tuning-fork-shaped" earthwork enclosure at O'Byams Fort site near Hickman, Kentucky is perhaps their most unique undertaking. It is clearly reminiscent of the Hopewellian style, and their unique pottery has been found at Hopewell sites in Ohio, such as Seip Earthworks, Rockhold, Harness, and Turne.

Havana Culture

Centered in Illinois but extending into the Mississippi valleys of Iowa and Missouri, some anthropologists believe the Havana Hopewellian Culture is ancestral of the Mississippi Culture, while others think it is an ancestor of the Cahokian people. Believed to have established themselves by 200 B.C., the Havana are most often associated with the Toolesboro Mound Group, a group of Havana Hopewell earthworks on the north bank of the Iowa River east of

Wapello, Iowa. The Havana built numerous conical-shaped mounds, with Mound #2 at Toolesboro measuring 100 feet in diameter and 8 feet in height. It is possibly the largest mound in Iowa.

Kansas City Hopewell Culture

By 300-100 B.C., the Kansas City Hopewell established themselves at the very western edge of the Hopewell Interaction "Sphere" and overlapped the subsequent Mississippian Tradition. The Kansas City Hopewell Culture was intricately linked with Hopewellian development, settling a number of large villages and smaller occupational camps in Kansas and Missouri around the mouth of the Kansas River, with 30 recorded Kansas City Hopewell sites remaining today. With an economy based on horticulture (corn/maize, squash, and marsh elder), as well as hunting and gathering (deer, fish, turkey, nuts, and wild seeds), the Kansas City Hopewell was directly interconnected with the Hopewellian trade system.

Kansas City Hopewell mounds typically have central stone tombs that contain cremated human remains. Exemplified by the Trowbridge and Cloverdale sites near Kansas City and Saint Joseph, the Kansas City Hopewell excelled in a distinctive style of pottery evolving from "cord-wrapped" to "dentate stamping", which consisted of combinations of punctates (tool or fingernail marks) and trailed lines. They also had "crosshatched" decorations.

Significant Hopewellian Monumental Sites (Groups of Burial Grounds with Extensive Enclosures)

M. C. Hopewell, Mound City, Harness, and Seip Groups (Ross County, Ohio)

Turner (Hamilton County, Ohio)

Tremper (Scioto County, Ohio)

Fort Ancient (Warren County, Ohio)

"Works" (Marietta and Newark, Ohio)

Regional effigy variants and other atypical sites include the earthen serpent found in Adams County, Ohio, the alligator effigy mound in Granville, Ohio, and earthen representations of buffalo, moose, fox, wolves, panthers, and lynx found in Wisconsin. These effigy mounds extend from Dubuque, Iowa, north into southeast Minnesota, across southern Wisconsin from the Mississippi to Lake Michigan, and along the Wisconsin-Illinois boundary.

Chapter 5: The Great Hopewell Road

Although the hundreds of mound sites strewn across Ohio provide an insightful look into Hopewellian life and the Hopewellian Interaction Sphere, to date there is no evidence to suggest that the Ohio Hopewell exerted any particular control over other related societies. Instead, anthropologists assume Ohio represented a major hub of inter-regional Hopewellian trade that simply developed centuries before other pivotal sites. Even so, one question that persists in the minds of many scholars is whether the Hopewell attempted to impress upon their neighbors their particular social and spiritual values via a road network that established trade and commerce. Could a road have been established to promote a religious "pilgrimage"? Might the road that connected the Hopewell settlements at Newark and Chillicothe have established the supreme spiritual destinations for all native groups of North America?'

A growing number of scholars thinks the evidence makes it likely. In 1862, James and Charles Salisbury began a survey of a six-mile section of road "marked by parallel earthen banks" discovered near the Hopewell site at Newark, Ohio, and they soon noted that the road "appeared to extend much farther in the direction of Chillicothe." As anticipated, further exploration revealed that this road connected these two great Hopewellian centers, a distance of 60 miles through the heart of Ohio, and that it was likely built specifically for ritual processions. One present-day advocate of the Great Hopewell Road hypothesis, Dr. Bradley T. Lepper of Ohio State University at Newark, claims there are still traces of the road remaining at four additional places along the 60-mile line connecting the cities.

Deeming it the "Great Hopewell Road," historians, anthropologists, and Hopewellian scholars have since speculated what its larger purpose may have been, and many believe it was part of a much larger trade-route system. According to Dr. Lepper:

"Several sets of parallel walls which seem to create processional paths were part of the Newark Earthworks. One set of parallel walls extended southwest from the Octagon at the present site of 31st Street. In 1820 Caleb Atwater speculated that these walls went at least thirty miles. In 1863 James and Charles Salisbury traced them for six miles 'over fertile fields, through tangled swamps and across streams, still keeping their undeviating course.' The Salisbury brothers suggested the road might have linked Newark with the earthworks at Circleville or Chillicothe."[6]

Lepper has since determined that if the road did indeed continue on a straight southwest-northeast course, the so-called "Great Hopewell Road" would have led directly to Chillicothe, the center of Hopewell culture. He speculated, "Perhaps this road was a holy pilgrim's path like similarly long and straight roads built by the Mayan culture in Mesoamerica which they called 'sacbeob,' or 'white roads.' The people of the Hopewell culture may have followed such roads to the great earthworks centers bringing offerings of copper or mica as gifts as supernatural powers invoked by the monumental geometry of these sacred places."[7]

---

[6] Lepper, Bradley T. "The Great Hopewell Road and the Role of Pilgrimage in the Hopewell Interaction Sphere." Page 122.

[7] Lepper, Bradley T. "Searching for the Great Hopewell Road."

Although conclusive physical evidence of the Great Hopewell Road has yet to be uncovered, Lepper has presented infrared aerial photographic images to support this hypothesis, recently stating, "As opportunities arise, I continue to sift through the archives of museums and historical societies for references to earthen walls and ancient roads. In addition, I'm still finding and studying new (and old) aerial photographs of the landscape between Newark and Chillicothe. It is clear that the plow-flattened walls show up best under particular soil conditions, for photographs of the same area taken at different times of the year sometimes reveal traces of the walls and sometimes do not. In 1931, Warren Weiant, Jr. noted the lines in the soil could be seen only during a short period of time in the spring--apparently the grass grew more slowly on the soils comprised of the earthwork remnants."[8]

If Lepper's hypothesis is correct, a walled "Road" some 65 yards wide and 56 miles long once ran directly from the octagonal "observatory" at Newark to its astronomical counterpart at Chillicothe, specifically to accommodate Hopewellian astronomer-priests who routinely charted the skies. Lepper and a growing number of other prominent scholars and historians contend that religious ascetics could easily have found the Hopewell complex on the Scioto River from points south by "following the long-assumed north-south trade routes, then following the so-called 'pilgrims' path' northeastward to the Great Circle and Octagon at Newark."[9]

In keeping with the "pilgrimage" scenario, Lepper asserts that although travelers and pilgrims may have used the long-proposed travel route to bring exotic goods to the spiritual centers of Ohio, the most important thing taken away was a deepened spirituality, thereby creating a system that was ultimately incumbent on ceremonial syncretism and shared belief. And while the true purpose of the so-called "Great Hopewell Road" may never be known, evidence would suggest that much more than material wealth was traded among peoples of the Hopewellian Tradition. In fact, these societies may well have accomplished an ideological meeting-of-the-minds, the likes of which has never been seen before or since across North America.

While a vast amount of physical evidence supports the contention of a "Hopewellian Interaction Sphere" that extended to a number of groups centered in South Carolina, Georgia, and Alabama, it was only in recent decades that the final few dots connecting the Ohio Hopewell with indigenous groups as far south as Tampa Bay, Florida were added. Since that time, however, the names Weeden Island, Tocobaga, and Manasota have become regular components of the Hopewell/Mound Builder discussion.

Much of what is known today about the Hopewell/Florida connection was first suggested by archaeologist and Florida scholar C. B. Moore, who in the late 19th century conducted extensive studies of known Hopewellian mounds in north Florida. This was followed a half-century later by archaeologist William Sears, who began intensive excavation at the Green Point (on Florida's

---

[8] Lepper, Bradley T. "Searching for the Great Hopewell Road."
[9] Lepper, Bradley T. "Searching for the Great Hopewell Road."

northwest coast), Crystal River (now Crystal River State Park), Yent (near St. Teresa), and Pierce (near Apalachicola) complexes. Sears ultimately established the Florida/Hopewellian "type site" and grouped particular archaeologically-recognizable traits into a complex he termed "Yent."

With artifacts uncovered at Crystal River, Yent, and Pierce, including copper panpipes, silver-plated copper earspools, animal jaw bones, gorgets, carnivore teeth, and human hand designs, Sears was able to scientifically established a definitive relationship between the Yent (Swift Creek) complex and Hopewell mounds of Ohio and Illinois, as well as Hopewellian earthworks of the Southeast. Additionally, bowls excavated from all three sites with distinctive flat "T-shaped" lips directly correspond with many found at the Seip Mound in Ohio, further demonstrating the Swift Creek/Ohio Hopewell connection. Taken full circle, an intact Crystal River pot with a distinctive "check-stamped" design was recovered at Mound City in south-central Ohio, shell plummets of a Yent-complex design were found at Seip, and conch shells found at Turner, Seip, and Hopewell are of obvious Florida Gulf Coast origin.

Evident by the vast array of artifacts now uncovered and radiocarbon-dated, indigenous Floridians and peoples of the North and Southeast maintained long-distance trade for millennia. Assumed to have been first initiated by the Adena and then advanced by Hopewellian societies seeking exotic goods from the Gulf Coast, Florida products (especially Busycon shells that could be crafted into cups, beads, and other ritual items) were apparently traded for northern copper, stone, and ceramics beginning around 100 B.C. Based on such trade, numerous Hopewellian-style mound centers were established by the 1st century A.D. in north-central Florida and the inland tri-state Alabama-Florida-Georgia area, with the emergence of the Swift Creek-Santa Rosa Hopewell Culture (100-800 A.D.) in northwest Florida attesting to the far-reaching influence of Hopewellian religious ideology. Although the Swift Creek-Santa Rosa coastal culture is not considered as influential on subsequent Florida cultural patterns as groups of the interior, anthropologists acknowledge two specific groups as cultural progenies of the Swift Creek Hopewell Tradition: the Weeden Island (300-900 A.D.) and Tocobaga (circa 800-1500 A.D.) near St. Petersburg and Tampa Bay, respectively.

Most scholars agree that the common use of Hopewellian mortuary artifacts across the eastern half of the present-day United States indicates large-scale trade, but the logistics, politics, and ultimate purpose of such a system has fostered a number of competing theories over the past century. For example, many scholars believe a political "network strategy" tied to elites, persons of status such as "Big Men" or Chiefs, was in place across the Hopewellian "sphere". In this system, exotic goods were given in reciprocal exchange or as social payment of debt, damages, bride-price, ceremonial function, or other signs of respect, as a form of tribute. Others contend that if such an exchange system did exist, it was directly related to shared religious beliefs that necessitated an ongoing procurement of ritual items. Still others support the view that pilgrims from various societies routinely traveled and made offerings of exotic goods as demonstrations of supplication or homage when visiting Hopewell ceremonial centers, thus bringing a steady flow of exotic goods north. Finally, others attribute the natural desire for exotic items as being responsible for the establishment of socioeconomic ties between neighboring villages and villages from other regions.

Chapter 6: The Legacy of the Mound Builders

By all indications, around 500 A.D. the Hopewell exchange system broke down, mound building ceased in northern regions, and art-forms were no longer produced. Simply put, the Ohio Hopewell began to fade from the North American landscape. Some scholars believe inter-regional war was the cause of their demise, and as evidence they point to the fact that numerous villages of the Late Woodland Period shifted to larger communities fortified with walls and ditches. Others believe that a colder climate, perhaps even a mini-Ice Age, drove wildlife away and detrimentally effected vegetation, resulting in an overall reduction in food and other resource availability. Some further speculate that the widespread use of the bow and arrow further exacerbated the food shortage.

Maybe there are entirely different reasons for the disappearance of the Hopewell. As cultural anthropologists Robert Dunnell and Diana Greenlees suggest, the Hopewellian Tradition may have suffered disintegration due to a widespread breakdown in societal organization resulting from full-scale agriculture. This argument is premised on the idea of waste behavior: "energy was diverted from biological reproduction during a period when climate irregularities favored small families. As climate became predictable from year to year, energy was turned from waste behavior to food production."[10]

While the true cause of their collapse may never be known, most scholars do not consider their disappearance from the cultural scene the end of their influence. In fact, many consider it just the beginning. Since the adherents of the Hopewellian Tradition had no apparent written language, and no Hopewellian culture survived into modern times, almost everything we know or assume we know about Hopewell society is based on scholarly speculation derived from the body of physical evidence left behind. From an academic perspective, the crux of that scholarly speculation rests on the probability of an advanced society with ritual behavior at its core. But even with tens of thousands of artifacts and physical remains to examine, there is no scientific way to quantifiably verify that what appears to be ritual behavior actually reflects Hopewellian religious views, or even if those views were universal across the entire Hopewellian sphere of influence.

One of the greatest and most controversial challenges facing archaeologists today is attempting to identify ritual activity in the archaeological fossil record, based off the artifacts, structures, trash, plant and animal remains, and other material culture found at archaeological dig sites.

---

[10] Dancey, William "The Enigmatic Hopewell of the Eastern Woodlands." Page 131.

Naturally, none of these sites have artifacts that explicitly explain their purpose, leaving archaeologists with the task of trying to categorically distinguish utilitarian artifacts from ceremonial ones. This was a challenge beyond the purview of most archaeologists of the past, but in recent years, a number of cross-discipline specialists known as "cognitive anthropologists" with mixed concentrations in psychology, sociology, religious practices, and ancient history have emerged from the field of anthropology. These specialists are educated in recognizing the so-called "signs."

While prehistoric ritual behavior is rarely self-evident, cognitive anthropologists recognize that people worldwide express religious beliefs in very similar manners, particularly in artistic expression. Thus, the preponderance of ornate necklaces, beautiful carvings of bone and wood, exquisite earspools and pendants, intricately designed pipes, masks, and finely-crafted items of pearl, copper, and silver commonly found in Hopewellian funerary settings can reasonably be equated with ritual behavior. A number of quite exquisite pieces recovered from burial mounds, such as a rare mask using a human skull as a face plate found at Mound City, an ornate pipe portraying a dwarf, and an 11" x 6" human hand cut from a single sheet of mica also lend credence to this presumption.

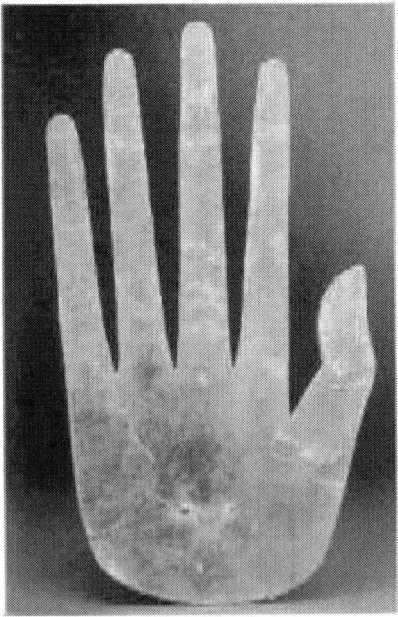

The carved mica hand

Of all the items typically found in Hopewellian mounds, smoking pipes are historically most directly associated with religious and ritual activity. First appearing in the archaeological record during the Late Archaic Period (1500-1000 B.C.), pipes seem to have become integral to ceremonial life during the Early Woodland Period (1000-1 B.C.), along with the advent of "smoking" rituals and pipe-carving techniques. Among the Ohio Hopewell, elaborately carved stone "platform" pipes were most common, while large elbow types made of clay or stone seem to have been preferred by southern groups like the Swift Creek in Tennessee, Georgia, South Carolina, and north Florida. Especially significant to scholars is the fact that even though pipes were common throughout the eastern part of North America, they are very rarely found outside a mortuary setting, thus supporting the ritual designation.

While there is no clear consensus among American anthropologists concerning the presence of shamans or holy men in Hopewellian society, many support the likelihood based on particular artifacts and artistic renderings found in many settings. One such example is a pipe excavated from Mound City depicting a bird-man. A bird with the head of a man is thought to illustrate "soul flight," the trance-like state induced by shamans around the world by a number of means, including the smoking of various herbs, during which the holy man is transformed into a bird or carried away by a bird. Similarly, the stone "Wray Figure" found at Newark depicts a human virtually enveloped by a bear, not as if being devoured but as though he is becoming the bear by first donning its costume. Typical of many cultural traditions around the world, these motifs are frequent subjects of artistic expression and commonly assumed to have a ritual connection, especially when found in funerary settings. Thus, while many aspects of Hopewellian life remain subject to debate, physical evidence of their religious beliefs and rituals is seldom challenged.

Even at the most fundamental level, the Mound Builders' cultural tradition was nothing short of phenomenal. In addition to the fact that they established the first society-level cooperative on the North American continent, the Adena and Hopewell promoted a sedentary, communal lifestyle through shelter construction and the establishment of permanent villages. From there, they established widespread horticultural practices, promoting corn, beans, and squash cultivation, they were responsible for the advancement of crafts and technology, including stone and bone tool-crafting, leather working, and cloth production, and they created and sustained an extensive synergistic trade network that handled the constant flow of crafts, foodstuffs, and natural resources over tens of thousands of square miles. Given the time periods in which the Mound Builders accomplished all of this, they managed to create cross-cultural cooperation on an unprecedented scale, with unprecedented results.

Although the methods by which these peoples accomplished everything is still unclear, most scholars believe it was the direct product of ritual practices first established by the Adena (reflected in their mortuary practices) and then advanced by the Ohio Hopewell, who took the practices to a monumental scale. And while this all-inclusive societal organization undoubtedly spawned untold sociological, intellectual, and technological advances (which historically benefited European settlers as well), most scholars agree that it was the Mound Builders' ritual practices that ultimately had the greatest social impact, as seen among the religious observances of Native American societies all across the continent.

By the time Europeans arrived in the early 16th century to colonize what would become the United States, there were an estimated 1,000 different Native American tribes inhabiting America. Among these were two of the Mound Builder Tradition, the Natchez (descendants of the Plaquemine Culture near present-day Natchez, Mississippi) and the Shawnee (descendants of the Fort Ancient Culture). Although geography, climate, social interactions, war, and the passage of time all resulted in a variety of worldviews, traditions, and spiritual belief systems among the tribes, a spiritual commonality evolved amongst all indigenous Native American groups: the notion that the people shared a close bond with the earth. Spirituality occupied the core of their lives.

As a result, no matter which Native American tribal religion one studies today, he or she will find ritual elements from the Mound Builders at its core. As early as 2500 B.C., the Adena institutionalized a number of spiritual traditions that not only survived into modern times but even remain essential elements of current Native American ritualism. For example, effigy pipes were common features of Adena burials and Hopewellian burials, and they remained a key component of Native American ceremonialism, with numerous groups (including the Algonquian, Cherokee, and Cheyenne) developing elaborate pipe-crafting and tobacco-smoking ceremonies. Similarly, Adena funerary cults and the practice of including broken pottery with the dead have carried over into modern times, with Puebloan and Navajo cultures of the Southwest honoring this ancient custom well into modern times. And of course, animal symbolism common to both Adena and Hopewellian ritual settings is now central to all Native American spiritualism, expressed both materially and conceptually in craft motifs (on pottery, baskets, pipes, and other arts), song and dance, traditional folk stories, the concepts of "spirit animals" and "spirit guides," totem depictions, and Native American mythology. All of these forms of expression, including the mythology, almost certainly reflect tales and mythology that were derived from the Mound Builders.

Expanding on Adena ceremonialism, the Hopewellian Tradition formalized a number of religious customs, including the wearing of headdresses to denote power and authority. This was perpetuated among many Native American tribes, from the simple gustoweh cap of the Iroquois to the buffalo horn headdress of the Sioux. The inclusion of "trophy" skulls in burials was a common practice found in Puebloan funerary rituals well into the 20th century. And the formation of an astronomer-priest sect, like those believed to have been monitoring the skies at Newark and Chillocothe, effectively established the "seer," making them a forerunner of the holy man and shaman found among so many Native American cultures.

The Mound Builders' ritual elements were further advanced by the Mississippian Mound

Builders, who instituted religious cults that are exemplified by the Hopi Kachina Cults of today. The use of cosmic imagery to link legendary warrior-heroes engaged in supernatural acts is a common motif of most Native American mythology, and calendrical observances like the Green Corn Festival are reenacted annually by dozens of Native American groups, including the Cherokee, Muscogee, and Ojibway. The concepts of priests possessing supernatural powers and the designation of "sacred ground" are common to all Native American groups.

The physical remains of the Mound Builders and the mysteries surrounding them will continue to fascinate societies and keep scholars busy, but for those trying to determine the Mound Builders' lasting legacy, they need look no further than North America's Native American tribes. Put simply, the Mound Builders initiated, established, and promoted the spiritual ideology, rituals and customs that evolved into formal Native American religion, making them the common forefather of all the continent's Native American tribes.

Bibliography

Adovasio, J. M. and Jake Page. The First Americans: In Pursuit of Archaeology's Greatest Mystery. *New York: Random House, 2002.*

Byers, Martin A. The Ohio Hopewell Episode: Paradigm Lost and Paradigm Gained. *OH: University of Akron, 2004.*

Dancey, William. "The Enigmatic Hopewell of the Eastern Woodlands." In North American Archaeology. *Loren Malden: Blackwell Publishing Ltd., 2005.*

eText.Virginia.edu website: "Jefferson, Thomas, 1743-1826. Notes on the State of Virginia." Accessed via: http://etext.virginia.edu/toc/modeng/public/JefVirg.html 01.17.2013.

Fagan, Brian. The First North Americans: An Archaeological Journey. *London: Thames & Hudson, 2011.*

Hicks, Ronald. "The Great Hopewell Mystery." In Archaeology, *52:76, November/December 1999.*

Hodge, Frederick. Handbook of American Indians North of Mexico. Smithsonian Institution Bureau of American Ethnology Bulletin 30. *New York: Greenwood Press, 1969.*

Lepper, Bradley T. "The Great Hopewell Road and the Role of Pilgrimage in the Hopewell Interaction Sphere." In Recreating Hopewell, *pp 122—133. Gainesville, Florida: University Press of Florida, Gainesville, 2006.*

"Searching for the Great Hopewell Road." Accessed via: http://ww2.ohiohistory.org/ohiojunction/hopewell/research.html 01.20.2013.

Lorenz, Karl. *"The Natchez of Southwest Mississippi."* In Indians of the Greater Southeast: Historical Archaeology and Ethnohistory, *pp. 142--177. Gainesville: University Press of Florida, 2000.*

Milner, George M. The Mound Builders:Ancient Peoples of Eastern North America. *London: Thames & Hudson, 2005.*

McCulloh, James H., M.D. An Attempt to Settle Some Points Relative to the Aborigines of America. *Baltimore, MD: Joseph Robinson, 1817. Accessed via : http://olivercowdery.com/texts/1817McC1.htm#title 01.18.2013.*

Moss, Joyce and George Wilson. Peoples of the World: North Americans. *New York: Gale Research, Inc., 1991.*

Natchez Nation website: http://www.natcheznation.com/ Accessed 01.21.2013.

Neusius, Sarah, W. and G. Timothy Gross. Seeking Our Past: An Introduction to North American Archaeology. *Oxford: Oxford University Press, 2007.*

O'Donnell III, James, H. Ohio's First Peoples. *Ohio: Ohio University Press, 2004.*

Official Website of the Shawnee Tribe: http://www.shawnee-tribe.com/ Accessed 01.22.2013.

Salisbury, James A. and Charles Salisbury. *"Accurate Surveys & Descriptions of the Ancient Earthworks at Newark, Ohio."* American Antiquarian Society, *Worcester, Massachusetts, 1862.*

SnowOwl.com, "Natchez People" website: http://www.snowwowl.com/peoplenatchez.html Accessed 01.21.2013.

Waldman, Carl. Encyclopedia of Native American Tribes. *Oxford: Facts on File Publications, 1985.*

Warren, William W. History of the Ojibway People. *St Paul, MN: Minnesota Historical Society Press, 1984.*

Made in the USA
Lexington, KY
17 June 2016